# The Jungle
## *Coloring*
## *Book*

# The Jungle
## *Coloring*
## *Book*

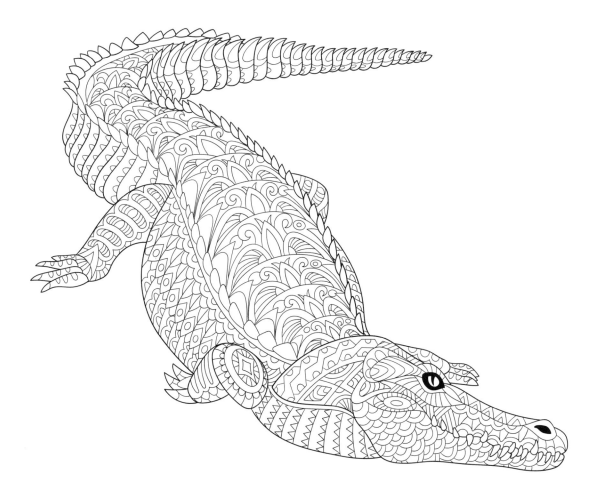

SIRIUS

**SIRIUS**

This edition published in 2024 by Sirius Publishing, a division of
Arcturus Publishing Limited,
26/27 Bickels Yard, 151–153 Bermondsey Street,
London SE1 3HA

ISBN: 978-1-3988-4039-3
CH011160NT

Printed in China

# Introduction

Jungles and rainforests, with their abundant plant life and fascinating animals, are found all over the world, in central Africa, the Indian subcontinent, in many parts of south-east Asia, and South America. Each has its own specific climate and wildlife. Jungles tend to have dense, tangled vegetation at ground level, while the rainforest canopy allows limited sunlight, so lower level plants do not flourish in the same way. Both support a wonderful array of different animal, bird, and plant species, many of which are pictured in this coloring book. You'll find big cats including tigers and leopards, huge herbivores like hippos and elephants, and graceful primates such as tarsiers, lemurs, orang-utans, and various monkeys. There are vivid hummingbirds, gorgeous birds of paradise, parrots, and toucans—as well as the trees and other plant life found in a jungle or rainforest. Take a selection of brightly colored pencils, pens or markers, select your favorite quiet place and spend a couple of hours coloring your own corner of the jungle.

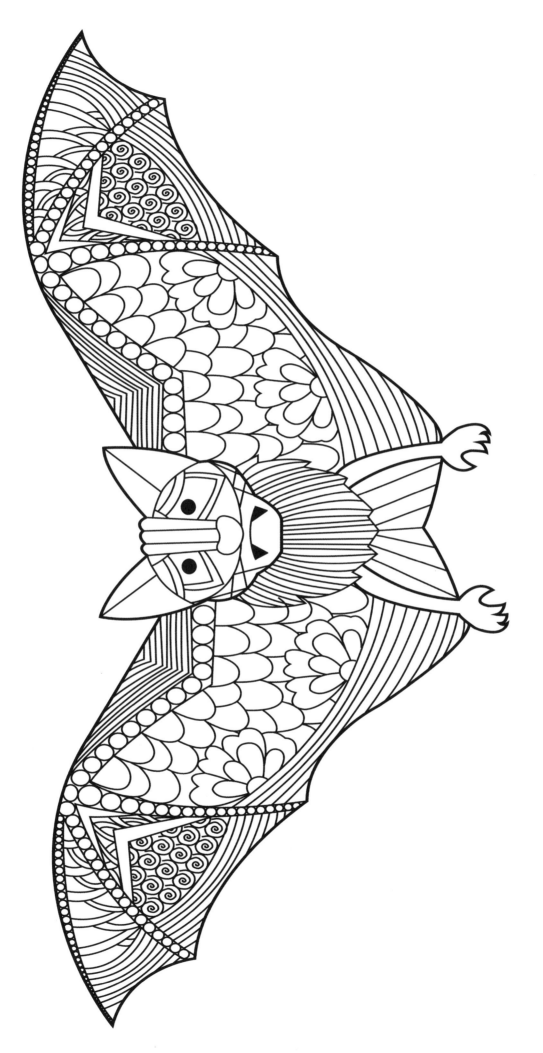

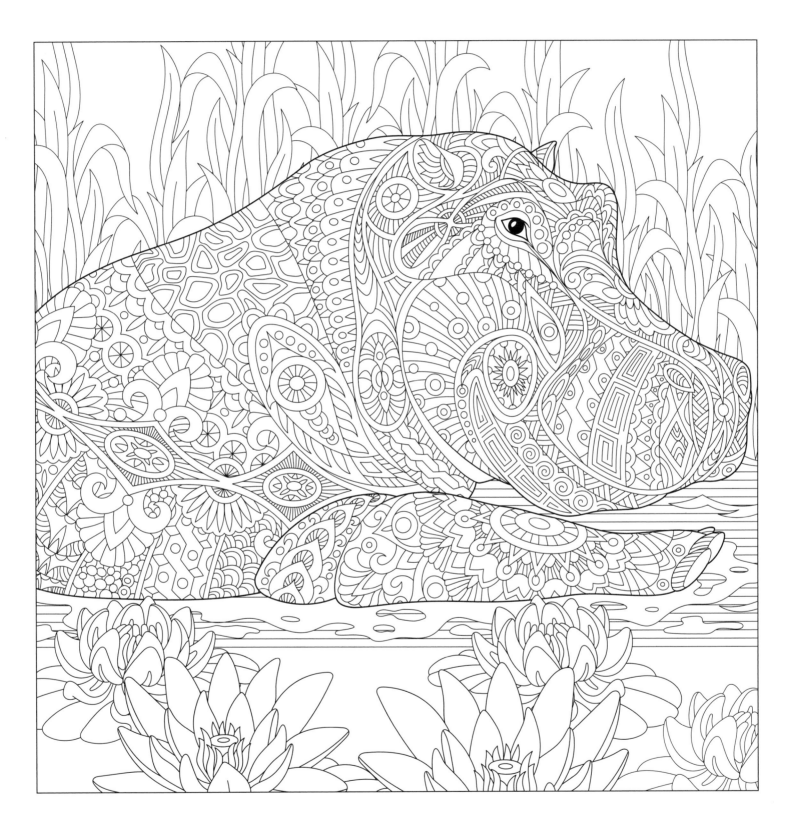

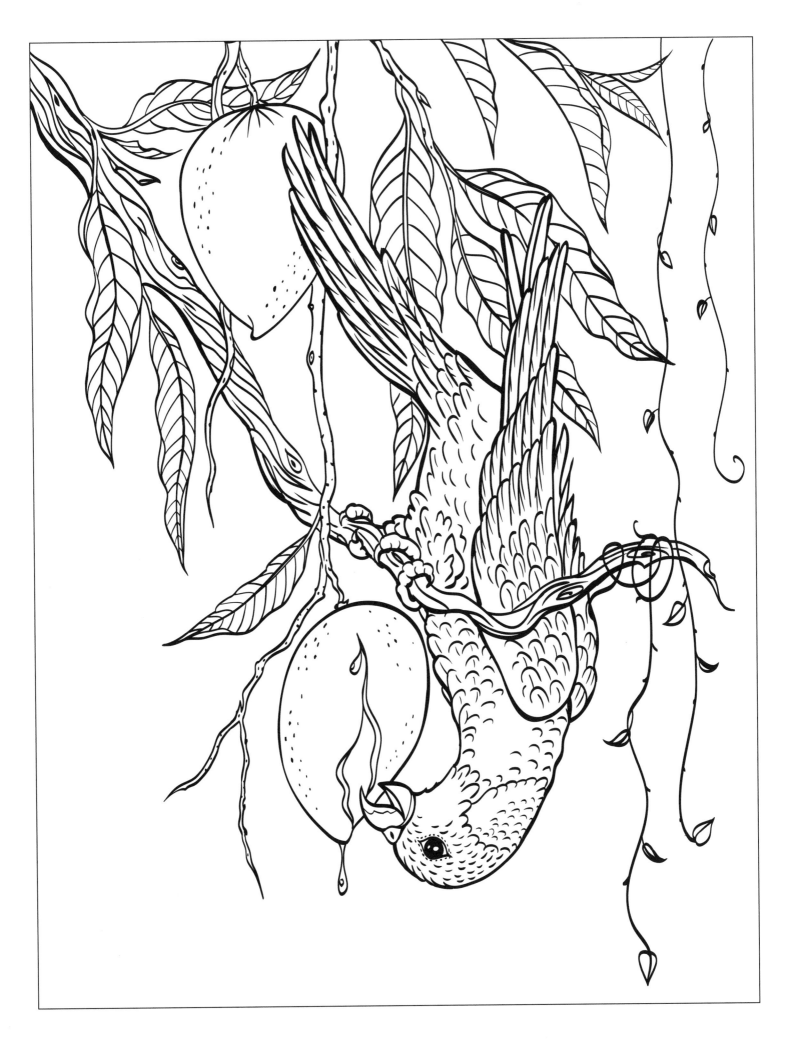

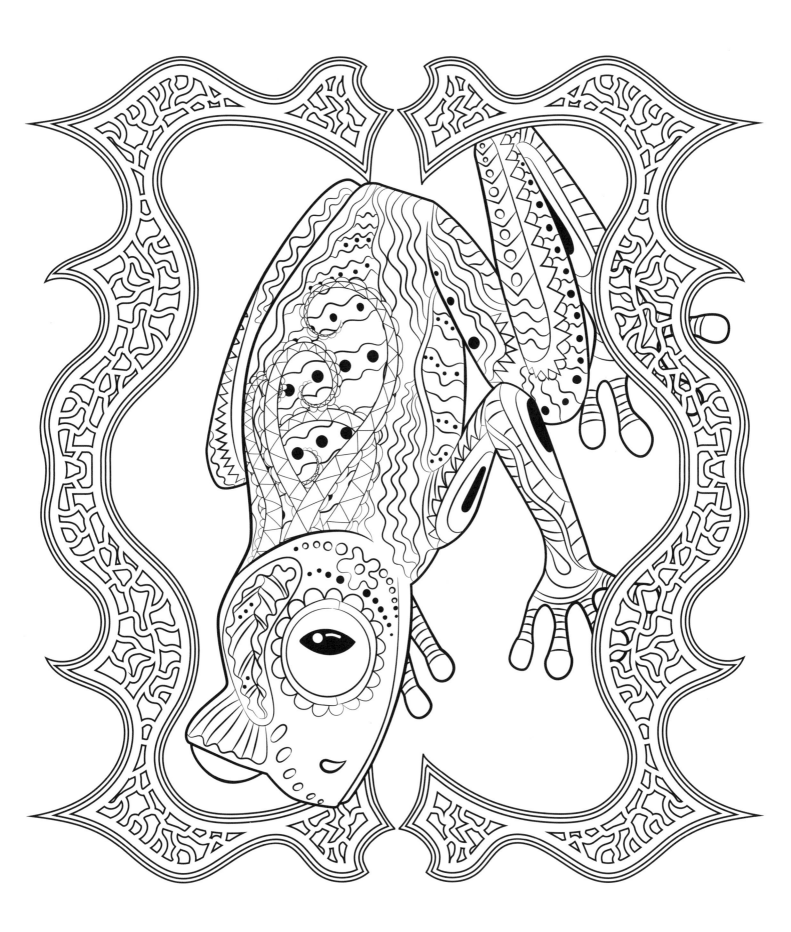

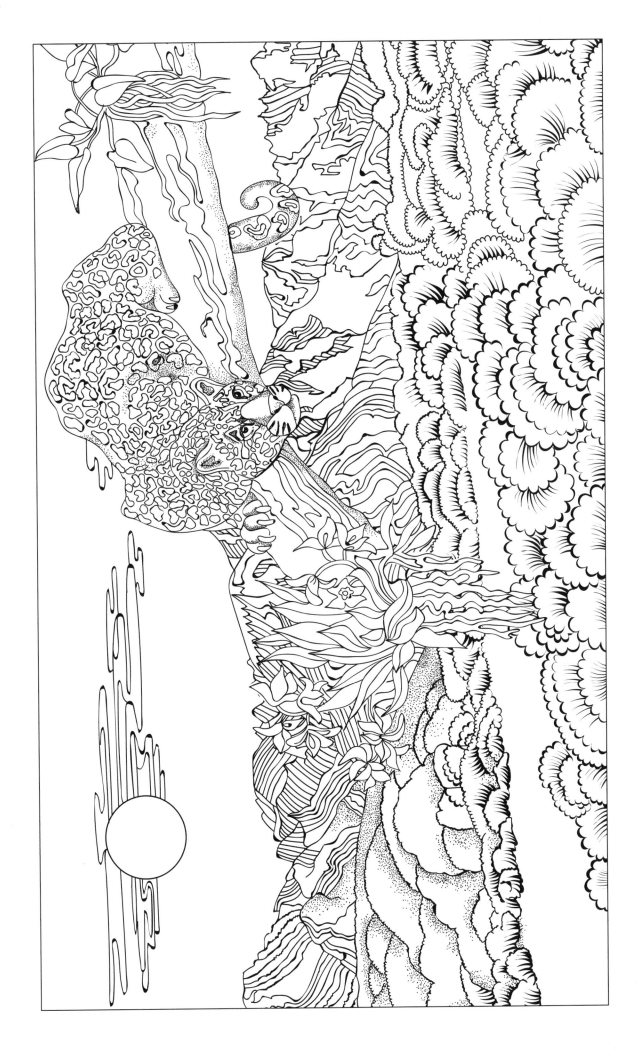

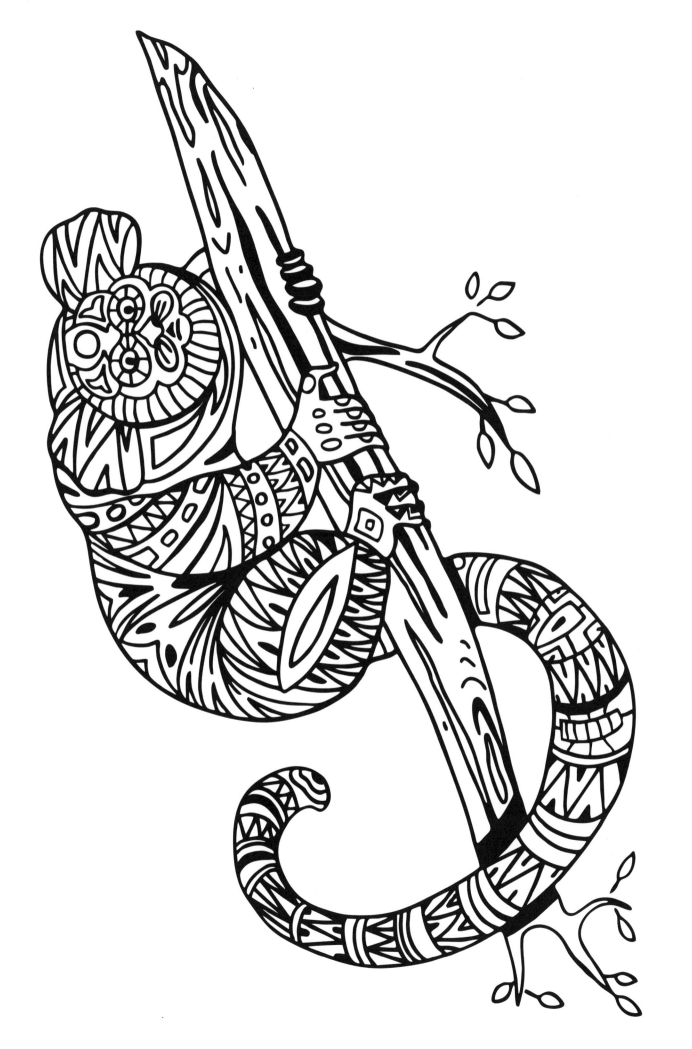